OUR WORLD IN CRISIS

HEALTH & DISEASE

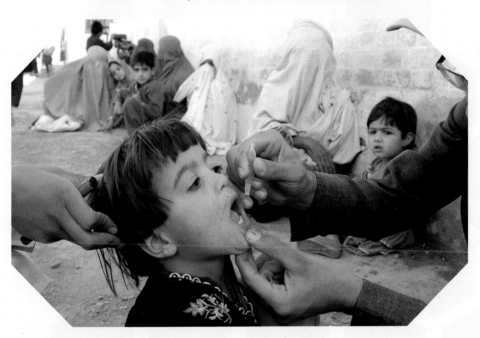

IZZI HOWELL

W
FRANKLIN WATTS
LONDON • SYDNEY

Franklin Watts
First published in Great Britain in 2018 by The Watts Publishing Group
Copyright © The Watts Publishing Group, 2018

Produced for Franklin Watts by
White-Thomson Publishing Ltd
www.wtpub.co.uk

ISBN: 978 1 4451 6377 2

Credits
Series Editor: Izzi Howell
Series Designer: Dan Prescott, Couper Street Type Co.
Series Consultant: Philip Parker

The publisher would like to thank the following for permission to reproduce their
pictures: Alamy: ECHO cover and 31, Sunil Sharma/Xinhua/Alamy Live News 29, age
footstock 32; Getty AAGGraphics 12, AFP/AFP 17, SIA KAMBOU/AFP 19, Mario
Tama 21, s-dmit 23, Victor J. Blue/Bloomberg 35, Ashley Cooper 36, BSIP/UIG
43; Shutterstock: Asianet-Pakistan title page and 25, Master Video 2 and 42, Vlad
Karavaev 5, Michelle D. Milliman 6, kurhan 9, Mat Hayward 10, testing 14, Robby
Fakhriannur 15, Linda Parton 16, Attila JANDI 27, Travel Stock 38, BlurryMe 40,
humphery 44, Prometheus72 45.

All design elements from Shutterstock.

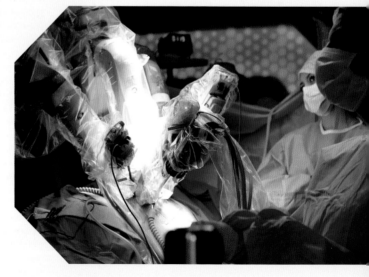

Printed in Singapore

Franklin Watts
An imprint of
Hachette Children's Group
Part of The Watts Publishing Group
Carmelite House
50 Victoria Embankment
London EC4Y 0DZ

An Hachette UK Company
www.hachette.co.uk
www.franklinwatts.co.uk

CONTENTS

What are

HEALTH & DISEASE?

Feeling healthy is something that people can take for granted. Many people in high-income countries normally feel fine and can easily access healthcare if they feel ill. However, health problems have a significant impact on the well-being, and even life expectancy, of many people in low- and middle-income countries.

What is health?

According to the World Health Organization (WHO), health is 'a state of complete physical, mental and social well-being and not merely the absence of disease or infirmity'. Health is about feeling good most of the time, not just being free from infectious diseases, such as the flu, or health conditions, such as diabetes. Most people around the world do not fit into this category of good health.

Measuring health

One way of assessing the health of people in an area is by looking at their life expectancy at birth. Healthy people have longer life expectancies than people with health problems. The world average life expectancy at birth is currently 69 years. However, women across the world live longer than men, with a female life expectancy at birth of 71.1 years compared to just 67 years for men.

High-income countries tend to have longer life expectancies than low- and middle-income countries. This is because low- and middle-income countries do not always have the resources to keep their citizens healthy. The health of people in these countries is negatively affected by lack of access to clean water and medicine, food insecurity and poor living conditions. Many babies and children die from conditions relating to poverty, which brings down the country's life expectancy.

Lack of access to clean drinking water threatens the health and lives of millions of people around the world, such as these children in Kenya.

AVERAGE LIFE EXPECTANCIES AT BIRTH (2016)

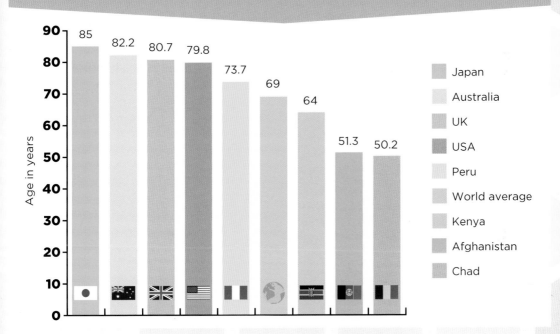

Age in years

Japan
Australia
UK
USA
Peru
World average
Kenya
Afghanistan
Chad

CASE STUDY

Life expectancy in Japan

Japan is a high-income country with a powerful economy and generally high standards of living. Japanese people have an average life expectancy at birth of 85 years, which is one of the highest in the world. This is partly due to the fact that over 93 per cent of the population live in cities, with access to clean water, sanitation and healthcare facilities. Japan also spends a large amount of its budget on guaranteeing healthcare for its citizens. The traditional Japanese diet is thought to be extremely healthy, with plenty of fresh fish and vegetables.

Geography

Some of the poorest countries in the world are found in hot areas near to the equator in Africa, south-east Asia and South America. These areas are home to certain diseases that do not occur naturally in cooler regions, where countries tend to have higher incomes. For example, the mosquitoes that carry malaria and the Zika virus only live in tropical areas. The lack of funds available in low- and middle-income countries makes it challenging to control the spread of these diseases.

Tropical countries are also more likely to experience extreme weather conditions that affect agriculture. If a crop is destroyed, people in the area may not have enough money to buy more food. Not having enough food to eat leads to malnutrition (not receiving enough nutrients) and eventually starvation. People suffering from malnutrition are weakened and find it harder to fight off additional diseases.

Many children in Haiti are suffering from malnutrition after a hurricane destroyed their harvests. A swollen belly is a sign that a person is not consuming enough protein.

Diseases around the world

People in high-income countries are usually affected by different diseases than those who live in poorer countries. Many people in low- and middle-income countries die from infectious diseases, such as diarrhoea and HIV/AIDS. Residents of high-income countries mainly suffer from non-communicable diseases that they develop as a result of lifestyle choices, such as heart disease and diabetes.

TOP 10 CAUSES OF DEATH IN LOW- AND HIGH-INCOME COUNTRIES

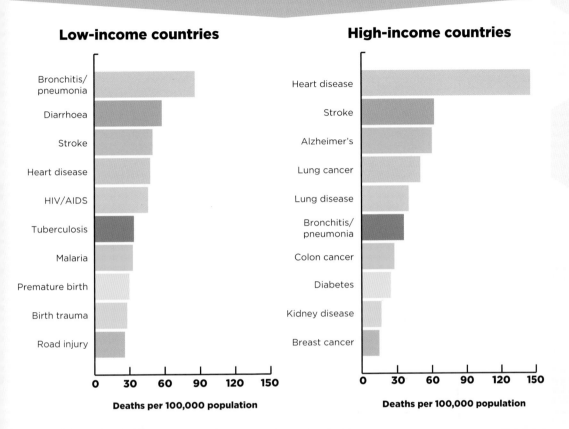

Low-income countries

Bronchitis/pneumonia	
Diarrhoea	
Stroke	
Heart disease	
HIV/AIDS	
Tuberculosis	
Malaria	
Premature birth	
Birth trauma	
Road injury	

0   30   60   90   120   150

Deaths per 100,000 population

High-income countries

Heart disease	
Stroke	
Alzheimer's	
Lung cancer	
Lung disease	
Bronchitis/pneumonia	
Colon cancer	
Diabetes	
Kidney disease	
Breast cancer	

0   30   60   90   120   150

Deaths per 100,000 population

Healthcare strategies

Each country needs to have a different healthcare strategy, based on the particular needs of its population. Governments look at data, such as leading causes of death, to decide how best to invest public money in healthcare. In low- and middle-income countries, ensuring that all citizens have clean drinking water would stop many unnecessary deaths. However, this is proving to be difficult due to lack of funding and the logistical problems of supplying water to remote rural areas.

In high-income countries, healthcare providers need to encourage people to make lifestyle changes to prevent diseases such as heart disease. However, this is easier said than done, as people struggle to prioritise exercise and make healthy choices.

Leading a healthy lifestyle is key to maintaining good health and living a long life. Eating a balanced diet, keeping fit, sleeping well and avoiding harmful drugs and alcohol will help you to feel your best.

Food

Eating is one of the most important ways of staying healthy. Food contains calories, which give the body energy to carry out its daily functions and keep the internal organs working. The number of calories that we need per day depends on our age and activity level. Adults need more than children, and people who are active need more than people who do not move around much. Eating more or fewer calories than the body needs can lead to health problems.

A balanced diet

A balanced diet is made up of a mixture of different food groups, such as carbohydrates, protein, fat, vitamins and minerals. We need to eat more food from some groups than others. For example, we need to eat more carbohydrates than fat. Sugar and salt should be eaten in moderation as too much can damage your health. People who do not eat a balanced diet may become underweight or overweight, which can lead to additional health problems.

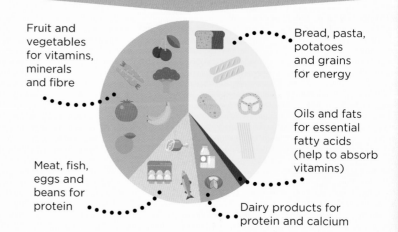

A BALANCED DIET

Fruit and vegetables for vitamins, minerals and fibre

Bread, pasta, potatoes and grains for energy

Oils and fats for essential fatty acids (help to absorb vitamins)

Meat, fish, eggs and beans for protein

Dairy products for protein and calcium

A HEALTHY LIFESTYLE

Obesity

Eating more calories than the body burns can lead a person to become overweight or obese. Some people also have medical conditions that lead to weight gain. Obesity around the world has doubled since 1980. In 2014, 39 per cent of the world's adults were overweight. Being overweight leads to health problems such as diabetes and strokes. Currently, more people die from being overweight or obese than from being underweight.

Body Mass Index

One way of calculating if someone is a healthy weight is by looking at their Body Mass Index (BMI). A person's BMI is calculated by dividing weight in kilograms by height in metres squared. For adults, a BMI of 18.5 to 24.9 is considered healthy, 25 to 30 is overweight and above 30 is obese. However, the BMI system has been criticised as the formula does not take muscle weight into account. Many muscular people are incorrectly categorised as overweight, due to the weight of their muscles. For this reason, BMI works best as a general indicator of health, rather than a precise reading.

Measuring waist to hip ratio is another way to identify obesity in adults. The waist measurement should be smaller than the hip measurement.

What can you do?

Speak to someone at home or at school if you are worried about being overweight or underweight. Lead an active life and try to eat food that is rich in protein, carbohydrates and vitamins and minerals. Cut down on sugar, saturated fat and salt.

Active lives

According to the British National Health Service (NHS), young people should be doing an hour of exercise every day, such as walking or sport. However, many people today do not achieve this target. It is very easy to rely on technology to do physical things for us – for example, driving instead of walking and watching TV rather than playing physical games.

Benefits of exercise

Leading an active life has many health benefits. Moving your body burns calories, which helps to reduce the risk of obesity. Exercise also strengthens your bones and muscles and releases endorphins, which put you in a better mood. For adults, regular exercise cuts the risk of diseases such as heart diseases and cancer by up to 50 per cent.

Exercises in which you have to support your body weight, such as swinging from bars, help to strengthen your body.

Sleep

Getting a good night's sleep can influence your health as much as your diet and the amount of exercise that you do. Children who don't sleep enough are more likely to be overweight or obese, as they often get their energy boost from sugary foods. Children between the ages of nine and sixteen should be sleeping around nine to ten hours a night.

Keep your bedroom dark

Go to bed and wake up at the same time every day

HEALTHY SLEEP HABITS

Wind down by reading a book

No screens in the bedroom

Wear earplugs if it's noisy

Mental health

Mental health is a key part of our overall health. Our mental health can be affected in the short term by our surroundings and our relationships with others. Make sure you take care of yourself during difficult times by eating well, sleeping and doing things for fun. Some people are also affected by long-term mental-health disorders, such as depression and bipolar disorder. These people may need to take medication or receive treatment from a therapist to manage their condition effectively.

? What can you do?

It's normal to feel sad, angry or worried from time to time. If you feel low most of the time, talk to someone you trust at home or school. You can find out more information about mental health at https://youngminds.org.uk.

Substance abuse

There are several substances that can be harmful to our bodies. Some are always dangerous, such as cigarettes. Others, such as painkillers and alcohol, damage your body if you take too much. A few substances, such as cannabis, cocaine and heroin, have been made illegal because they pose such a serious threat to our health.

Smoking

Smoking tobacco kills around six million people every year. Up to half of smokers will be killed by health problems caused or made worse by their tobacco use. Tobacco contains nicotine, which is addictive and makes people want to smoke more. Cigarettes also contain carbon monoxide, which reduces the amount of oxygen that the blood can carry. This increases the risk of heart disease and strokes. The tar in cigarettes can cause cancer – smokers are at a high risk of lung, mouth and throat cancer.

Smoking also has a serious impact on people who breathe in second-hand smoke. Over 890,000 people a year die prematurely because of health problems caused by other people smoking.

Nearly 80 per cent of the billion people who smoke worldwide live in low- and middle-income countries, such as India.

What can you do? ?

Many young people feel pressured to try smoking or drinking alcohol. Practise beforehand saying 'no' confidently so that you are prepared if someone tries to pressure you.

Alcohol

Scientists say that adults can consume a limited amount of alcohol as part of a balanced diet. However, alcohol does have an impact on the body in the short and long term. Straight after drinking alcohol, a person may feel sleepy and less in control. Many years of drinking to excess does permanent damage to the brain and liver and can cause early death. Driving after drinking alcohol can cause fatal accidents.

Drugs

Illegal drugs such as cannabis, cocaine, heroin, LSD and ecstasy tend to be addictive and dangerous. One of the most serious risks is taking too much – a drug overdose can result in long-term health problems or even death. Drugs are sometimes mixed with other poisonous substances, which can cause instant death. As illegal drugs aren't regulated, users do not know exactly what they are taking.

ILLEGAL DRUGS AND HEALTH RISKS

Cannabis – mental-health problems, such as depression

Ecstasy and cocaine – damage to the heart and nervous system

LSD and magic mushrooms – mental-health problems, such as psychosis

Aerosols and glue – damage to the brain

Ketamine – damage to the bladder

Heroin – damage to the lungs

A HEALTHY ENVIRONMENT

The quality of the air we breathe, water we drink and the land on which we live and grow crops plays an important role in our overall health. Nearly one in four deaths around the world can be attributed to an unhealthy environment.

Air quality

Air quality has a huge impact on health – outdoor pollution causes the deaths of an estimated 3.7 million people every year globally. Much of the air pollution comes from industry, traffic and fossil fuel power plants. These sources release gases, some of which contain microscopic particles that we breathe in unknowingly. Once inside our body, these particles increase the risk of developing cancer and lung disease.

CASE STUDY

Pollution in China

China emits a huge amount of air pollution through its heavy use of coal power stations, cars and rubbish incineration. The gases released form thick smog over towns and cities. People wear face masks and build domes over outside sports facilities to avoid breathing in the polluted air. Around one-third of all deaths in China can be linked to pollution, which makes it roughly as deadly as smoking.

Improving air quality

Many countries have signed agreements promising to reduce the amount of pollution released, such as the Paris Agreement. However, this is voluntary and there are no consequences if countries don't meet their target. Furthermore, some of the most polluting countries, such as the USA, have not signed new agreements and have even pulled out of the Paris Agreement.

Housing

If a property is not ventilated properly, it can become damp and mouldy and so its residents are more likely to develop allergies and asthma. Indoor air pollution is also a serious problem in low- and middle-income countries, where people often cook over coal or wood stoves. The gases released by the cooking fuel can cause breathing problems and certain types of cancer, if the room is not ventilated properly.

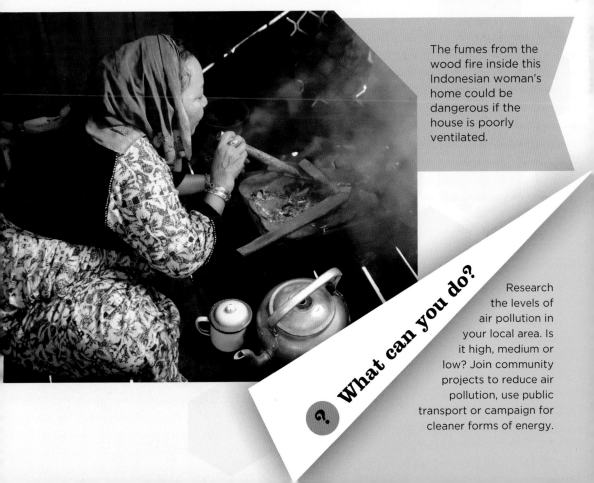

The fumes from the wood fire inside this Indonesian woman's home could be dangerous if the house is poorly ventilated.

What can you do?

Research the levels of air pollution in your local area. Is it high, medium or low? Join community projects to reduce air pollution, use public transport or campaign for cleaner forms of energy.

Drinking water

Rural areas in low- and middle-income countries may not have a source of clean drinking water. Instead, people in these communities depend on water from rivers and lakes. This water may contain harmful bacteria, parasites and human waste.

Sanitation

Correct disposal of human waste (urine and faeces) is key to ensuring good health. If human waste pollutes the water supply, people using the water can develop diarrhoea and more serious diseases, such as cholera. Around the world, 2.4 billion people are at risk of poor health due to poor sanitation.

At least
1.8 BILLION
people use a drinking water source that is contaminated with faeces.

- - - - - - - - - - - - - - - -

Almost
900
children die every day from diarrhoea caused by dirty water and poor sanitation.

CASE STUDY

- - - - - - - - - - - - - - - -

Drinking water in Flint, Michigan

It is not just low-income countries that have problems with clean drinking water. The city of Flint, in the state of Michigan in the USA, has not had clean tap water since 2014. State employees changed the water supply to save money and started extracting water from a dirty water source, which was not treated properly to make it safe for human use. The water that flows from residents' taps is poisoned with iron, lead and other toxins. Those who can afford bottled water use it to drink, cook and bathe, but many people do not have the money to do so. People who have been exposed to the water have developed lead poisoning and are suffering from rashes and hair loss. Lawsuits have been brought against those responsible, but the situation has not yet been resolved.

Volunteers hand out bottled drinking water in Flint, Michigan.

Pesticides and fertilisers

Pesticides are toxins used to kill insects and other pests that might damage crops or carry diseases. Although pesticides can be useful, they are toxic to humans and can cause health problems for those who work and live near them. Artificial fertilisers, used to make crops grow better, also contain chemicals that are harmful to health.

Some people prefer to avoid the risk by eating organic food, which has been grown without pesticides and artificial fertilisers. However, even if you only eat organic food, tiny particles of pesticides and fertilisers remain in the air and can be breathed in. When it rains, pesticides and fertilisers run off into rivers and become part of the main water supply.

Accidents

Keeping workers in dangerous industries safe is important. Many people in low- and middle-income countries work in deadly factory conditions where they are exposed to poisonous fumes and chemicals. Some companies do not invest in safety equipment or training for their staff, as they prioritise profit over their workers' safety.

CASE STUDY

The Bhopal disaster

In 1984, 45 tonnes of toxic gas escaped from an insecticide factory in Bhopal, India, and spread over nearby residential areas. Thousands of people were killed immediately when they breathed in the poison gas. 500,000 survivors now suffer from respiratory disorders and eye problems as a result of the gas they inhaled. The company did not pay to have the factory cleaned properly, and the toxic gas polluted the soil and water. Even though the accident happened over thirty years ago, babies are still being born with birth defects due to the pollution left behind.

This survivor of the Bhopal disaster lost her sight because of the toxic gas leak.

DISEASES

Infectious diseases, such as tuberculosis and flu, are caused by pathogens – micro-organisms that cause disease. Non-communicable diseases, such as diabetes and heart disease, are due to various factors, such as genetics, lifestyle or conditions during pregnancy.

Bacteria

Bacteria are a type of pathogen that can live inside or outside the body of living things. Once inside a body, bacteria can release poison that makes the person feel ill. However, not all bacteria are bad. Some are harmless and many play important roles inside the body, such as the bacteria in the digestive system that help to digest food. The average adult male has around 40 trillion bacteria in his body, most of which live in the digestive system.

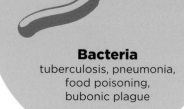

Bacteria
tuberculosis, pneumonia, food poisoning, bubonic plague

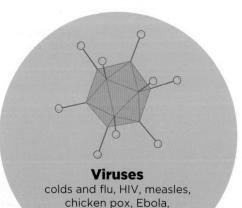

Viruses
colds and flu, HIV, measles, chicken pox, Ebola, some types of pneumonia

Viruses

A virus is a very small pathogen. When a virus enters the cell of a living thing, it reproduces and damages the cell. The reproducing virus spreads across other cells, damaging them as well. This process makes the living thing feel ill.

Fungal diseases

Fungi are a family of living things that includes mushrooms and mould. Some small fungi are pathogens and can cause serious diseases in humans. Once inside the body, certain fungi can release toxins that cause types of pneumonia, meningitis and allergic reactions. Fungi can also irritate the skin.

Fungi
ringworm, athlete's foot, yeast infections, some types of pneumonia and meningitis

A doctor in the Ivory Coast treats a toddler for pneumonia. Pneumonia can be caused by bacteria, viruses or fungi.

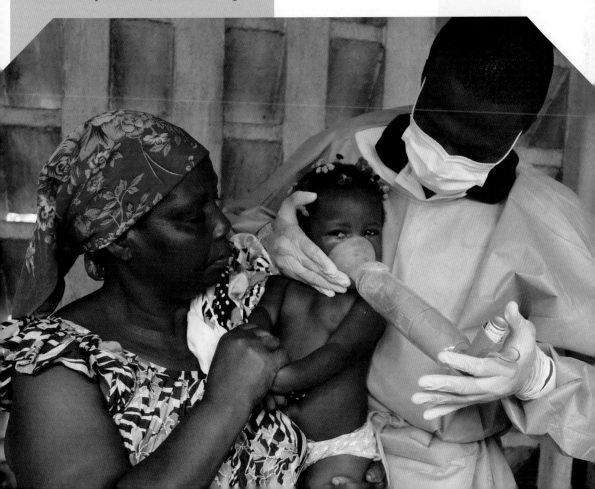

Genetic conditions

Mutated genes that are passed down from parents to children can lead to certain medical conditions, such as cystic fibrosis and breast cancer. Both parents need to carry the mutated gene for their child to be affected. The parents who carry the genes may not be affected in any way by the genetic condition, but their children may be.

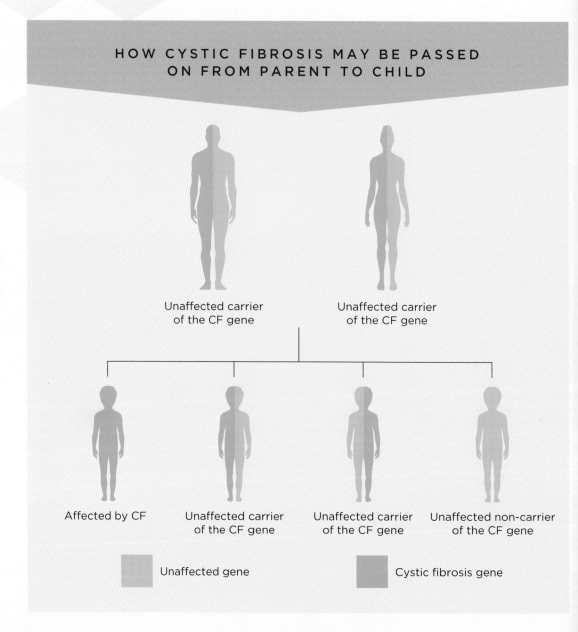

HOW CYSTIC FIBROSIS MAY BE PASSED ON FROM PARENT TO CHILD

Unaffected carrier of the CF gene

Unaffected carrier of the CF gene

Affected by CF

Unaffected carrier of the CF gene

Unaffected carrier of the CF gene

Unaffected non-carrier of the CF gene

Unaffected gene

Cystic fibrosis gene

Genes and chromosomes

Some genes can randomly change and mutate, leading to certain genetic conditions. For example, Down's syndrome is caused when an embryo randomly develops an extra chromosome. Around one in every 1,000 babies are born with Down's syndrome every year.

Pregnancy and birth

If a woman is exposed to chemicals, alcohol or tobacco during a pregnancy, there is a higher chance that her child will go on to have health conditions. For example, the children of women who smoked during pregnancy are more likely to develop asthma. Health conditions can also be caused by a difficult birth. If a baby does not receive enough oxygen during the birth, this can lead to conditions such as cerebral palsy.

CASE STUDY

Pregnancy and the Zika virus

Zika is a virus that is spread by mosquito bites. It is common in tropical regions, such as South America and the Caribbean. The Zika virus does not pose a major risk for people in good health. However, if a pregnant woman catches the disease, there is a risk that her baby will be born with microcephaly (a much smaller head). The small head size means that the baby's brain cannot develop normally and the child may have learning difficulties.

This baby in Recife, Brazil, was born with microcephaly as a result of the Zika virus.

Lifestyle-related conditions

Many deadly diseases can be directly linked to lifestyle choices, such as diet, smoking and activity levels. Up to half of long-term smokers will be killed by diseases linked to tobacco, such as cancer and lung disease. Maintaining a healthy weight through diet and exercise is proven to delay or prevent people from developing Type 2 diabetes. Type 2 diabetes can lead to further health conditions, such as blindness and heart attacks.

FIGHTING DISEASES

There are different ways to fight back against a disease. The body can fight diseases itself using its immune system. However, we sometimes need to use medicines to treat, cure and prevent diseases.

Getting inside

The body has several defences to stop harmful pathogens getting inside. It is hard for microorganisms to pass through thick skin. If the skin is cut, the blood clots and forms a layer to stop pathogens from passing through into the bloodstream. The strong acid found in the stomach usually destroys pathogens in food or drink.

Immune system

If a pathogen does manage to enter the bloodstream, the next stage of defence is the body's immune system. White blood cells from the immune system eat and destroy pathogens, such as bacteria and viruses. The white blood cells also produce antibodies that destroy pathogens.

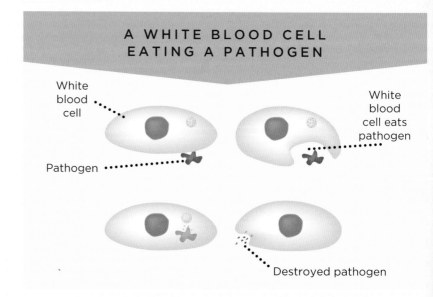

A WHITE BLOOD CELL EATING A PATHOGEN

White blood cell

White blood cell eats pathogen

Pathogen

Destroyed pathogen

Active immunity

Some antibodies remain in the body after the pathogen has been destroyed. If the same pathogen infects the body again, the white blood cells will be able to make more antibodies very quickly and destroy the pathogen more easily. This is called active immunity. Some parents deliberately expose their child to less harmful diseases while they are young so that the child develops active immunity for the rest of their life.

Chicken pox is uncomfortable for children but can be deadly in adults. If children catch chicken pox while they are young, they will have active immunity to protect themselves as adults.

Antibiotics

Antibiotics are a type of medicine that can kill bacteria by stopping them from multiplying. Penicillin was one of the first antibiotics to be developed and used to treat bacterial infections in the 1940s. Today, doctors treat infections with many different types of antibiotics. Antibiotics are only effective against bacteria and therefore cannot be used to treat viruses, such as the common cold.

Bacterial resistance

Bacteria can become resistant to antibiotics through the process of natural selection. Any bacteria that have randomly mutated to not be affected by the antibiotic will survive and go on to reproduce, creating more bacteria with the same resistance.

Overusing antibiotics and not completing a full course of antibiotics increase the chance of creating resistant bacteria. The only way to treat antibiotic-resistant bacteria is to develop new antibiotics, which is a long and expensive process.

CASE STUDY

MRSA

MRSA is a type of bacteria that is resistant to most antibiotics. This makes it incredibly hard to treat MRSA infections. Around one in 30 people carry MRSA bacteria on the surface of their skin without any symptoms. If MRSA gets deeper into the skin, it can cause mild infections, but if it gets inside the body, it can develop into a serious, life-threatening infection. MRSA commonly affects people staying in hospitals, as they often have exposed wounds through which the bacteria can enter. Hospital patients often have a weakened immune system from fighting other diseases, which makes it harder for them to defend themselves against MRSA.

Treating viruses

It is much harder to develop medicines that target viruses rather than bacteria. Scientists have managed to develop anti-viral drugs that improve the health and life expectancy of people with viral conditions, such as HIV. However, they have not yet managed to find a cure for this viral disease.

Viruses often mutate and change their genetic code. The body will have no active immunity against the new mutated virus and will need to produce new antibodies to fight it off again. The common cold virus mutates regularly, which is why we catch colds again and again.

What can you do?

Avoid overusing antibiotics. Antibiotics should never be taken to treat a cold or flu, as these are viral diseases. Make sure you finish any courses of antibiotics.

Vaccines

Vaccines are one of the most effective tools in fighting disease. Vaccines are commonly used to protect people against measles, mumps, polio and tuberculosis. A vaccine consists of a very weak or harmless version of a pathogen that poses no risk to health. When the body is exposed to the vaccine, it makes antibodies that it will use to protect itself in the future. The number of antibodies in the body may decrease over time, so people sometimes need booster vaccines to make sure that they are still protected.

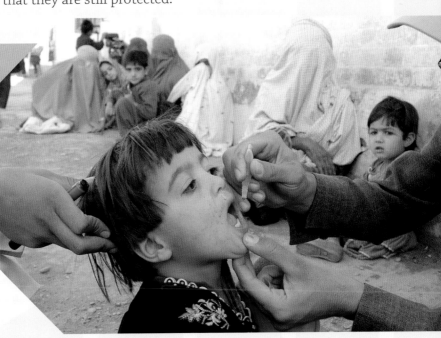

Drops of polio vaccine are given to a child in Pakistan. Vaccines can also be injected.

Vaccines prevent between
2-3 MILLION
deaths every year.

Polio has been wiped out in every country but
6
thanks to vaccines.

Around
19.4 MILLION
children worldwide have not received basic vaccines.

Traditional medicine

Some people treat diseases with traditional herbal medicines and treatments, such as acupuncture, that have been used for thousands of years.

In China, between
30 AND 50 PER CENT
of all medicines consumed are traditional Chinese herbal medicines.

Up to
80 PER CENT
of the population in Africa uses traditional medicine as their main source of healthcare.

Effective treatments

Traditional medicines can be effective treatments. Around 25 per cent of modern medicines are made from plants that were once used in traditional medicine. For example, the active ingredient in aspirin is extracted from the leaves and bark of the willow tree. It has also been proven that acupuncture helps treat migraines.

However, many treatments have not yet been proved to work. For example, scientists say that homeopathy is no more effective than a placebo (see page 27). A few vulnerable people have been deceived by false claims about the power of these treatments to cure conditions such as cancer. However, some people with mental health conditions, such as anxiety, are convinced that they work.

Research

There is still much research to be done on the effectiveness of other traditional medicines. It may be that there are many more traditional medicines that can be manufactured into modern treatments. However, scientists must test these medicines thoroughly and prove their effectiveness before they can be sold as new drugs.

Regulation

Some herbal medicines contain naturally toxic ingredients. These can damage the body rather than heal it if consumed in excess. It's important for traditional medicines to be regulated and controlled so that people know the correct dose of whatever they are taking.

This traditional Chinese medicine shop sells snake wine, made by infusing venomous snakes in alcohol. It is said to be good for vision and digestion, although there is no scientific evidence that it works.

Placebo effect

Scientists have discovered that in some cases, a patient's health can improve if they believe that they are taking medicine, while in fact, they are really being given a placebo – a substance that has no proven effect on heath. Researchers have observed how people suffering from pain, anxiety and depression have improved after being given a placebo treatment.

Placebos are very useful in medical research. Before a new drug can be sold, scientists must prove that the drug gives results that a placebo cannot. Some people believe that placebo trials are unethical, as the patients receiving the placebo may not benefit from the treatment. For example, in a study of a new cancer drug, only the patients given the real drug will receive actual treatment.

What can you do?

If you are interested in an alternative medicine treatment, always speak to your doctor first.

How
DISEASES SPREAD

Infectious diseases can be spread in many ways, for example via water, food, insect bites or through the air. Knowing how a disease is spread is crucial to prevent it turning from an outbreak into an epidemic.

Mosquito bites

Mosquitoes spread malaria and the Zika virus by sucking the blood of an infected person and carrying it to the next person that they bite. By using mosquito nets and spraying pesticides to kill mosquitoes, we can eliminate the carrier of the disease and stop it reaching humans.

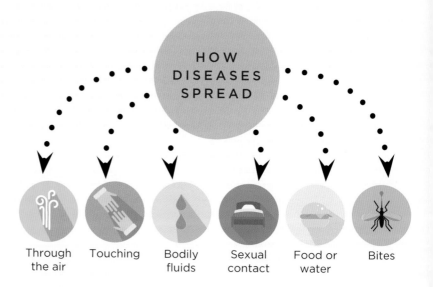

HOW DISEASES SPREAD

| Through the air | Touching | Bodily fluids | Sexual contact | Food or water | Bites |

Meat and fish

Some types of meat and fish carry dangerous pathogens. If these foods are cooked thoroughly, the pathogens are destroyed and the food is harmless. However, if you eat these foods raw or undercooked, you can contract diseases such as salmonella.

Students and teachers in Nepal wear face masks to school to protect themselves from swine flu.

CASE STUDY

1854 Broad Street cholera outbreak

Up until the 1860s, little was known about where diseases came from or how they passed from person to person. Many people believed that 'bad air' caused diseases such as cholera, when in fact, contaminated water was to blame. One of the first people to look into how diseases were spread was Dr John Snow, who traced a cholera outbreak to a water pump in the centre of London. His research into how the disease spread among the users of the pump convinced the authorities to shut it down, which led to the end of the outbreak.

Airborne

Airborne diseases, such as swine flu, spread quickly and easily, as it is hard to control the flow of air that we breathe. The tiny pathogens that carry disease are invisible to the naked eye, so we have no way of knowing what we are breathing in. Isolating ill people and wearing respirator masks keep people safe.

Epidemics

When a disease spreads quickly to many people at the same time, it is known as an epidemic. While some outbreaks are limited to a few countries, others spread around the world at an alarming pace.

What can you do?

Good hygiene helps to prevent diseases that are transmitted through touching, bodily fluids, food or water. Wash your hands frequently and cover your nose when sneezing.

Global travel

Diseases are spread across borders by travellers who are not aware that they are sick or travel in spite of their symptoms. Modern air travel means that a sick person can spread a disease to an area thousands of miles away in a matter of hours. In the past, it took longer for diseases to spread as people travelled more slowly on foot or by boat. Once an epidemic has spread to more than one country or area, it is known as a pandemic.

Basic reproduction number

Scientists use a figure called the basic reproduction number (BRN) to show how contagious a disease is. This number is an estimate of the number of new cases that will be caused by one person suffering from the disease. In theory, the higher the basic reproduction number, the harder it is to control an epidemic.

However, in locations with poor sanitation, diseases with relatively low BRNs such as Ebola (BRN 2) can sweep through a population, while countries with good-quality healthcare systems can control the spread of incredibly infectious diseases, such as measles (BRN 15), through vaccination and awareness campaigns.

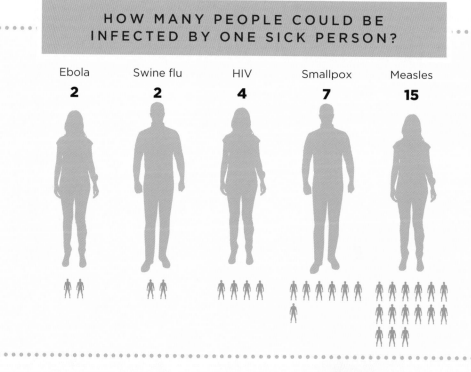

HOW MANY PEOPLE COULD BE INFECTED BY ONE SICK PERSON?

Ebola	Swine flu	HIV	Smallpox	Measles
2	2	4	7	15

Controlling an epidemic

There are several ways to bring an outbreak under control. Spreading awareness of how the disease is spread is key. Trained doctors and nurses may need to be brought into the area, if the local community does not have enough resources. Travel restrictions may need to be placed on the country to isolate the outbreak.

CASE STUDY

Ebola epidemic

In 2014, an outbreak of the Ebola virus in west Africa quickly turned into a two-year-long epidemic, which killed over 11,300 people. Close contact is needed for the disease to spread, as the virus is transmitted through the bodily fluids (blood, vomit or faeces) of someone with Ebola. Many people contracted the disease while nursing or burying Ebola victims, as traditional west African funeral customs include washing the body before burial. The epidemic initially got out of control because there were not enough resources to manage the outbreak. Volunteers who raised awareness about how to safely nurse and bury Ebola patients helped to slow down and eventually stop the virus.

Volunteers in biohazard suits prepare to safely bury an Ebola victim in Sierra Leone.

New epidemics

New diseases can sometimes appear as a mutation of a different disease or a disease that previously only affected animals. There is a serious risk of an outbreak of a new disease turning into an epidemic, as humans have little or no immunity to them and no scientifically tested treatments or cures. Diseases that have mutated so that they can be transmitted from animals to humans include swine flu and bird flu.

31

HEALTHCARE

INDUSTRIES

Healthcare is a booming industry that will always be in demand. Huge amounts of money change hands between patients, doctors, governments and pharmaceutical companies. However, some people argue that saving lives should be more of a priority than profit.

The right to healthcare

Health is a human right that applies to everyone in the world. This means that everyone has the right to receive good-quality healthcare, regardless of where they live or how much they earn. The WHO also believes that people should not have to put themselves into debt to receive healthcare – it should be free or reasonably priced.

Government spending

Some governments use tax money to provide free or cheap public healthcare for their citizens. Spreading the cost of healthcare across the population is cost-effective, as most people contribute more to the system than they take out. The amount of money that a government spends on public healthcare varies greatly around the world. Most of the countries with the highest rates of poor health and disease are low- or middle-income, which means that they have less government money to put towards healthcare.

SPENDING ON HEALTH PER HEAD IN US$

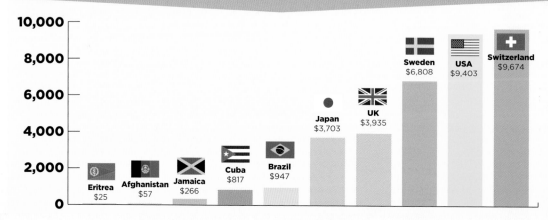

Eritrea	$25
Afghanistan	$57
Jamaica	$266
Cuba	$817
Brazil	$947
Japan	$3,703
UK	$3,935
Sweden	$6,808
USA	$9,403
Switzerland	$9,674

Funding healthcare

It is a challenge for most countries to finance public healthcare. Even if low- and middle-income countries dedicated more public money to healthcare, they would still not have enough to finance their needs. High-income countries can offer financial assistance to poor countries, so that they can afford to take care of their citizens.

High-income countries also struggle to find the money to keep up with their population's health needs and the cost of the latest technology and drugs. Countries can save money by switching to generic medicines (see page 35) and raise money by taxing unhealthy products, such as cigarettes.

Insurance and private healthcare

In some countries, individuals pay for private health insurance or receive it through their work. Some or all of their medical bills will be paid by the insurance company. Benefits of health insurance include being able to attend luxurious private hospitals, shorter waiting times for procedures and access to non-essential treatments, such as cosmetic surgery.

(see page 35)

CASE STUDY

Healthcare in Cuba

Despite widespread poverty, Cuba has one of the greatest free healthcare systems in the world. Its top priority is to keep Cuban citizens healthy and prevent illness, which is much cheaper and more efficient than trying to cure sick patients. Cuba has the third-highest ratio of doctors to patients in the world. Its many doctors knock on people's doors once a year for a check-up. Vaccines are compulsory and the state provides free transport to hospitals for people in rural areas. As a result, Cuba has the second-highest life expectancy in the Americas, while spending just US $817 per head.

Cuban doctors regularly visit the elderly and sick at their houses.

The pharmaceutical industry

The huge and powerful pharmaceutical industry researches, develops and produces drugs for profit. The drug development process is long and expensive. The average cost of bringing a new drug to the market is at least US $4 billion. However, pharmaceutical companies make huge profits from the sale of drugs and patents (the right to produce and sell the drug).

Research

Scientists are constantly researching ingredients and formulas that could be used to make new drugs. Some ideas come from traditional herbal medicines (see page 26), while others are inspired by different fields of research or random lucky discoveries.

Development

There are many stages of testing before a new drug can be distributed and sold. Once the formula has been thoroughly tested and found not to pose a significant risk, it is given to humans. The many stages of the development process add to the cost of developing the drug, but decrease the risk of a treatment with harmful side effects being distributed.

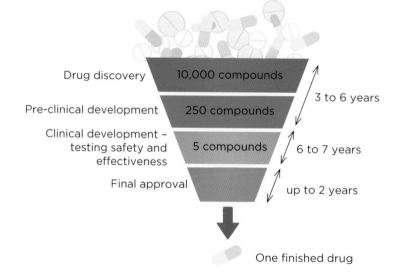

DRUG DEVELOPMENT PROCESS

Drug discovery — 10,000 compounds
Pre-clinical development — 250 compounds — 3 to 6 years
Clinical development – testing safety and effectiveness — 5 compounds — 6 to 7 years
Final approval — up to 2 years

One finished drug

Patents

Once a drug has been developed, the company that created it holds the patent for around 20 years. The company can easily charge a high price for it, as there are no other cheaper versions of the drug on the market to compete with. This makes many medicines too expensive for people who live in low-income countries or who don't have the income to buy the drugs themselves.

Generic medicines

Once a drug patent expires, other companies can make generic versions of the medicine. Generic medicines are identical to branded drugs in strength and chemical composition, but they are 20 to 90 per cent cheaper. This is because there are many varieties of generic drugs on the market, which creates competition and pushes the price down. Some people believe that large pharmaceutical companies should produce cheap generic versions of life-saving drugs before the patent expires, to save the lives of people who can't afford the branded version.

CASE STUDY

The price of Toxoplasmosis medicine

Toxoplasmosis is a relatively rare parasitic infection. Most cases are found in patients with weak immune systems, often as a result of AIDS. For them, the disease can be fatal. Up until 2015, the cost for a branded toxoplasmosis drug was US $13.50 (around £10) per pill. However, in 2015, a new pharmaceutical company bought the rights to the drug and increased the price by over 5,000 per cent, to US $750 per pill. The company argued that it was due to the high quality of the drug. However, this made the drug unaffordable for most patients in the USA. Many people considered this to be unnecessarily greedy, as a generic version is sold in the UK for under 50p a pill. The company has not yet lowered the price of the drug.

These protesters are protesting a rise in the price of EpiPens, a life-saving emergency treatment for people with severe allergies. The price of EpiPens has risen by nearly 500 per cent in the past few years, making them unaffordable for many.

Organisations such as the WHO work hard to improve health around the world. There are short and long term solutions that will help to make the situation better, including supplying medicines, training more doctors and tackling the global inequality that leads to health problems.

The World Health Organization

The WHO is a section of the United Nations that is dedicated to improving public health around the world. It works with governments around the world to target infectious and non-communicable diseases and improve conditions so that people can have the best possible health.

Aid

Medical charities, such as Médecins Sans Frontières, and certain governments from middle- and high-income countries, offer medical aid to countries that are in need. Medical aid consists of medicines, medical supplies and trained doctors and nurses, all of which are in great demand during emergencies such as epidemics. However, charities also provide long-term support for communities by giving medical training to local people, building healthcare facilities and campaigning for pharmaceutical companies to lower their prices.

Médecins Sans Frontières workers hand out malaria treatment to people in Malawi at risk of contracting the disease.

Education and awareness

Some communities have little formal education and poor awareness of how to prevent and treat diseases. They may blame their symptoms on witchcraft or bad spirits, and use traditional cures as treatment. Charities work around the world to raise awareness and help people protect and treat themselves correctly. There have also been successful awareness campaigns to encourage people to check for cancer and recognise the signs of a stroke. Early detection of these conditions helps to increase chances of survival.

CASE STUDY

HIV/AIDS awareness

HIV is a virus that gradually targets the immune system until the body can't fight off other diseases (a condition known as AIDS). There are currently nearly 37 million people living with HIV, mainly in low- and middle-income countries. However, the WHO believes that raising awareness and providing widespread treatment could mean the end of the AIDS epidemic by 2030. Once people know that the disease can be spread through unprotected sex, injections, blood transfusions or from a mother to her baby, they can change their behaviour accordingly to protect themselves. The WHO is also encouraging people to get tested for HIV, as many people are not aware that they carry the virus.

HIV/AIDS FACTS

Over 14 million people who are HIV positive do not know that they carry the virus.

New HIV infections fell by 33 per cent between 2000 and 2015.

Providing antiretrovirals to all people with HIV would prevent 21 million deaths from AIDS and 28 million new infections by 2030.

?. What can you do? Celebrate World AIDS Day on 1 December. Take part in events in your local area to raise awareness and fundraise for AIDS research and treatment around the world.

Access to healthcare

Many remote communities in low- and middle-income countries do not have healthcare facilities or local doctors and nurses. In an emergency, patients must travel a long distance along bad-quality roads to reach assistance. One solution to this problem is to set up mobile clinics that regularly visit remote communities or train local people in first aid and simple procedures.

Women in a remote village in India visit a mobile pregnancy clinic. Women in rural and poor communities are much more likely to die from complications during pregnancy or childbirth than women in rich, urban areas.

Social exclusion and health

Minority groups that commonly experience social exclusion, such as the Aboriginal population, Native Americans, Roma and Traveller communities, have higher rates of health problems and significantly shorter life expectancies than other groups of people. These minority groups often live in isolated areas with poor healthcare coverage and limited access to medication and fresh food. They often struggle to find well-paid jobs, which means that they may find it harder to buy healthy food or maintain a healthy lifestyle.

Investing money properly

A huge amount of money is invested into researching profitable drugs, rather than medicines that will help to save lives. Drugs needed in low- and middle-income countries are not profitable, as the people who need them cannot afford to pay a high price for them. One drug company stopped research into an Ebola vaccine in 2010, as it was not profitable. If they had finished trials of the drug, a vaccine might have been available at the beginning of the 2014 outbreak (see page 31) and could have prevented the virus from spreading so widely.

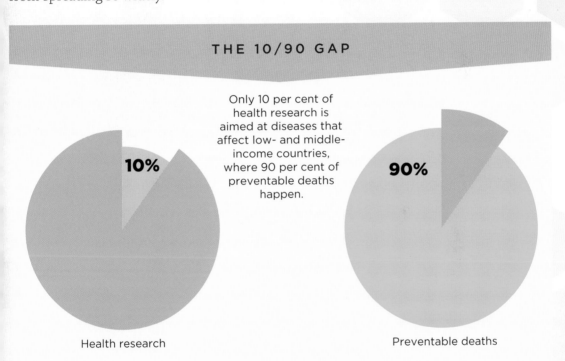

THE 10/90 GAP

Only 10 per cent of health research is aimed at diseases that affect low- and middle-income countries, where 90 per cent of preventable deaths happen.

10%

90%

Health research

Preventable deaths

Improving lifestyle

In high-income countries, rates of non-communicable diseases can be lowered by encouraging people to make lifestyle improvements. For example, in the UK, the NHS '5 A Day' campaign recommends that people eat five portions of fruit and vegetables per day, as research shows that eating enough of these foods can prevent heart disease and certain cancers.

The FUTURE

The medical research being done today will lead to a better understanding of vaccines, treatments and cures in the decades to come. However, our changing society brings new health challenges that we will need to tackle.

Eradicating diseases

When a disease no longer exists in an area, it is considered to have been eliminated. For example, polio has been eliminated from the USA since 1994. An eradicated disease no longer exists anywhere in the world. In 1980, smallpox was the first disease to be eradicated. It had previously killed three out of ten people who caught it. Scientists hope that we can eradicate many more diseases in the next decade, including polio, mumps and measles.

Insecticides are sprayed in Thailand to kill mosquitoes carrying malaria. Thailand is working towards eliminating malaria.

CASE STUDY

Eradicating malaria

Malaria is preventable and curable, yet there were 429,000 deaths from the disease in 2016, most of which were in Africa. The USA managed to eliminate malaria in 1951 by killing mosquitoes with insecticides, destroying their breeding grounds and treating malaria sufferers. Eventually, there were no malaria parasites in the human population for mosquitoes to transmit and the disease was eliminated. The Bill and Melinda Gates Foundation is using similar strategies, as well as developing new treatments, to try to eradicate the disease worldwide.

New cures

Scientists hope that they are close to finding cures for life-threatening diseases such as cancer, HIV/AIDS, Ebola and Alzheimer's disease. As well as investing money in research, it is important for countries to fund the training of new scientists to carry on the work in the future.

Genetic screening

Today, it is possible to screen embryos for genetic conditions and only select those that will not suffer from life-threatening diseases. This is seen as a positive step by carriers of genetic diseases who do not wish to pass on inherited conditions to their children. In the future, scientists may be able to screen for a wider range of diseases, including certain cancers, which will reduce the number of people suffering from these conditions.

Stem cells

Stem cells are a special type of cell found in embryos that can be grown to replace any other type of cell in the body. There is much ethical debate around the use of stem cells. This is because any stem cells used for treatment would need to come from a new cloned embryo, grown from cells from the person receiving the treatment so that their body's immune system wouldn't reject them. Some people consider that it is a valuable area of scientific research that could save many lives. Others disagree with the idea of creating new embryos that may eventually be destroyed after the stem cells are collected.

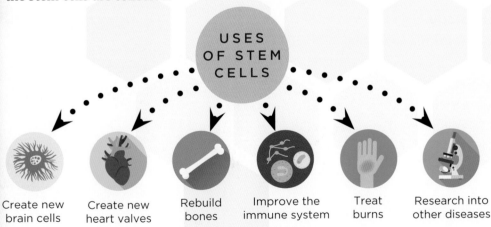

USES OF STEM CELLS

Create new brain cells | Create new heart valves | Rebuild bones | Improve the immune system | Treat burns | Research into other diseases

Robot surgery

Humans already use robots to assist in simple heart and colon surgeries, as they are more accurate and make fewer mistakes than human surgeons. These surgical robots are not yet fully automated – the surgeon guides the robot in case of an emergency. However, in the next decade or so, we may begin to use fully automated robots for simple operations. This would free up human surgeons for more challenging operations and bring down the cost, making healthcare more accessible.

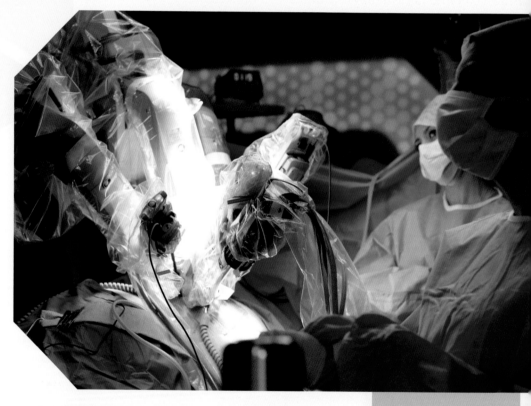

Doctors monitor an operation carried out by the Da Vinci surgical robot.

Nanotechnology

Nanotechnology is the development of very small robotic devices. A sheet of newspaper is 100,000 nanometers thick, while a nanorobot is between one and 100 nanometers. Nanorobots are small enough to travel in the bloodstream and could be programmed to target and destroy cancerous cells, and ignore healthy cells. We are probably less than ten years away from seeing this technology in use.

Personal monitoring

There has recently been a huge boom in wearable devices, such as Fitbits, that can monitor your health, including your activity levels, weight, heart rate and sleeping pattern. These relatively low-cost devices help people to evaluate their overall health and see the impact of their lifestyle choices without having to visit a doctor.

Wearable health monitors can also help people with long-term health conditions to manage their health. For example, a device that measures blood-sugar levels will help people with diabetes to choose the correct amount of medication. These devices can also carry out medical tests away from the hospital, which saves time and money and would be easier for patients in rural areas.

Bionics

Robotic devices used to replace human body parts are known as bionics. Bionics range from cochlear implants, which can allow some deaf people to hear, to bionic arms and legs that can be controlled by the brain. Scientists are currently working on a bionic eye for people with vision loss.

This man has great control over his bionic arm. He is demonstrating one of the events in the Cybathlon – a competition for people who use advanced bionic devices.

What can you do?

Try tracking your sleep patterns for a week. Write down when you go to sleep and when you wake up. Are you getting enough sleep? Look at the healthy sleep habits on page 11 for tips on how to fall asleep more quickly.

An ageing society

Advances in medicine have resulted in people living longer than ever before. Generally, this is a positive development, with people getting the chance to experience more and have longer with their families.

Diseases of age

However, people living longer does create certain challenges. As people grow older, they inevitably develop conditions related to ageing, such as hearing and sight loss, weakened bones and life-threatening conditions such as dementia. The increased number of people suffering from these diseases is putting extra pressure on healthcare resources and budgets.

Between 2015 and 2050, the number of people aged 60 and over will rise from

900 MILLION

to

TWO BILLION

These women live in a residential care home in China. Residential care homes for the elderly are one way of dealing with the health needs of an ageing population.

Age and population structure

In some countries, the population structure is changing so that a much higher proportion of the population is older. This is partly due to greater life expectancy, but also because falling birth rates mean that there are fewer young people in the country. In Japan, 30 per cent of the current population is over the age of 60. This creates an additional healthcare challenge, as there are fewer young people available to treat and care for a growing elderly population who may not be able to look after themselves.

Climate change

The rising global temperature will bring new health challenges. Insects and parasites will soon be able to survive in areas that were previously too cool, leading to new outbreaks of malaria. Periods of drought will affect agriculture and lead to food shortages and malnutrition. As well as trying to slow down and stop the progress of climate change, we need to create strategies to deal with these healthcare issues before it's too late.

Farmers around the world, such as this man in Turkey, are already losing crops to drought.

GLOSSARY

antibiotic – a medicine that destroys bacteria

antibody – a substance produced by the body to fight diseases

automated – something that is not controlled by humans

bacteria – a micro-organism that can reproduce inside or outside the body and cause disease

bionic – describes a robotic device that replaces a body part

birth rate – the number of babies born in a period of time

cell – the smallest part of a living thing

drought – a long period without enough rain

eliminate – to destroy a disease in an area

embryo – the cells that are beginning to become a baby human or animal

epidemic – a situation in which many people get the same disease at the same time

eradicate – to destroy a disease across the world

gene – a part of a cell that is passed on from parent to child and controls how the child will be

immune system – the parts of the body that fight off disease

infectious – describes a disease that can be passed from one person to another

life expectancy – the number of years that someone is likely to live

malnutrition – an illness caused by not eating enough nutrients

microorganism – a very small living thing

mutate – to change

natural selection – a process in which living things with genetic advantages have more chance of living long enough to reproduce and pass the advantage on to their children, increasing the rate of the genetic advantage in the population

non-communicable – describes a disease that can't be passed from person to person

parasite – a living thing that lives in or on another living thing and uses it for food

particle – a very small part of something

pathogen – a micro-organism that causes disease

pharmaceutical company – a company that develops and sells medicines

placebo – a fake medicine

profit – to make money by doing something

regulate – to control and check a process

sanitation – a system to remove dirt and human waste

toxin – something poisonous

vaccine – a substance that stops people from catching a disease

virus – a micro-organism that destroys cells

FURTHER INFORMATION

Books

Healthy for Life series
Anna Claybourne (Franklin Watts, 2016)

Living Forever: The Pharmaceutical Industry
Matt Anniss (Franklin Watts, 2015)

What's Next? The Future of Medicine
Lori Dittmer (Franklin Watts, 2013)

Websites

Find out more about health and disease on these websites:

www.dkfindout.com/uk/human-body/keeping-healthy/
Learn more about how to stay healthy

www.who.int/en/
Find out more about the World Health Organisation

www.ducksters.com/science/biology/viruses.php
Discover some amazing facts about viruses

INDEX

OUR WORLD IN CRISIS

  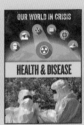   

W
FRANKLIN WATTS
LONDON•SYDNEY